The Gift of Life

Book of Poems

Through life's peaks with valleys....

One Day

Falling is felt
a large and dark hole
Wake up to shaking
loss of control

Though still I'm secure
awake in my bed
It's as if I'm still falling
reverberates in my head

This feeling it comes, it goes as it please
Not sure of alertness, conscious or dreams

Is this just a mark
a sign of duress,
Or is life simply slipping
toward my last breath

One day will I not
come awake from the depth
One day will I not
tumble-down like the rest

For I know the feeling of fallings most told
The spirit embodied, to have and behold

Who Comes Here

Who knocks at my door, felt a presence divine
in the midst of the night, awoke by a sign
As fear settles in, I've been here before
curiosity met, who awaits I'm unsure

The glow from outside as I move toward decision
awake or asleep what awaits my fruition

Inclined to invite, the path is now open
mind wanders silent, mistaken as focus
Thoughts toward promise, struggled through strife
Paid forward dues, what could only be right

Much to my wonder, behold it is I
the one you hold dearly, the one you prescribe
Dealt toward a knee, gasping last breath
pride at my door, when nothing is left

I wished for the world, only I could deserve
in vain I left conscience, gold as my word
Who knocks at my door, this shadow of me
the truth left unknown, awake from my dream

Edification

Ode to light
Shine decorum,
Filter perception
Decorate boredom

Graced by your presence
Circumvent life
Create silhouettes
Your body precise

Slayer of darkness
Virtuous nature
Your will grandiose
Pay elegant favor

Ode to beginnings
Morality ends
For once extinguished
Humanity condemned

Choice Of Faith

Puppeteer of life, placate us all
Claim not of choice, fate to befall

Each footprint that's left
already written
Choices unique
determination then given

Holy in spirit
of non believing
Sentence submitted
incubation for grieving

Which path will subdue me
render me whole
A choice if not mine
question my role

For whom have authority,
clouds now forsake me
To you I pay homage
return me now safely

The Lonely Tree

Testament of time, leaf on branch-

The bark of strength
roots beneath
Growth for miles
knowledge sleep

Passed by millions over generations
Lost of limb, regeneration

A living creature
took for granted
Breath to life
fulfill our planet

Home to wildlife
summer breeze
Shade from heat
admiration leaves

Fall of beauty
winter bare
No care, no worries
simply there,

The branch of hope
rest between,
Our greatest friend
the earthly tree

Flame In Time

Fire rage
throughout the night
Embers burn
one with light
Alone to self
I reminisce
White cloud of ash
a gentle mist

My mind is clear
no sound is heard
Restless still
the hours turn
Emotions felt
at every crackle
I feel myself
within its mantle

The warming fire
chill of breeze
Shivers sent
calming needs
I feed the flame
to my delight
The coals so hot
they reignite

I can not help
to see my youth
The kindling first
made from you
As you consume
all that's found
The troubled years
in me renowned

You as I
now prosper, rise
Until our fuel
runs out of time
We mustn't wait
count the days
The clock now ticks
our flame awaits

Cloud Away

The clouds paint pictures, sculptured ark -

The rain continuous
fall to earth,
The puddles form
consent of birth

While each unique
around the globe
We see an image
emerge, behold

Ever swift
its flow of motion
Change of color
valiant potion

Stare befuddled
for in this art
A world away
a world apart

Society Neglected

Body tired, shelter missing
Heart of gold, melt to missing

Coldness constant, lurk in shadows
Sadness hidden, beneath the shadows

Mislead to future, parents looking
While child fears, no one is looking

Left to those, the undesired
Prey on weakness, those undesired

From bad to worse, once good people
Steal to feed, a fear of people

Habit form, loss of reason
Aimless steps, with ghostly reason

Judgement made, now left unknown
No longer cared for, name unknown

Kings Throne

Cold and repugnant
stain within strife
Will never amount
or succeed in this life

Dead or in jail
not worthy of effort
A waste of humanity
societies leper

Destined for failure
why bother to try
A waste of a birth
your mother denied

Not made of necessity
ashamed of your valor
Aborted by choice
thus resembles your character

These words that I've chosen
description of you,
Are meant to make more
disappointment renewed,

Father you've spoken
your grave will not visit
Raised through the ashes
I lifted my spirit

The dungeon you left
understanding now why
Your weakness in knowing
your throne would be mine

Angry Forest

A lonely raindrop
upon my arm
Look to north
the scent of storm

In the woods
amongst the trees
To some a danger
I will not flee

The leaves grow quiet
state of calm
Now lightning strike
it won't be long

Thunder shake
the earth grow loud
It's power felt
vibrations sound

The wind then whispers
as if by chance
It's language heard
by common man

With anger now
for my distrust
This violent rage
a force of thrust

First lonely drop
upon my arm
Fuse with thunder
lightning storm
For in itself
won't signal fury
Combined as one
element of mercy

Destiny Speaks

Three days have past, since premonition
A chilling thought, now clouds my vision,

Await this moment, with bated breath
Mystique of destiny, will speak correct

A knock was seen, upon my door
No more is known, now insecure

Three days have come, I can not know
I can not rest, nor grasp control

Fear of loved ones, ill or harmed
Chills to bone, for I 've been warned

Three nights have past, when I'm awoken
Knocks on my door, I feared this moment

I take a breath in disbelief
for at the door, police in grief

Event Horizon

Event horizon
draws me close
A place of vastness
large in scope

My time here limited
cannot escape
No place to hide
silence my fate

An aura of beauty
now surrounded
Ironic this beauty
will soon devour

Event horizon
I give myself
Challenge you not
this hand was dealt

Ocean Sense

What a sight
that lays before me
The edge of the rock
an ocean story

Collect my thoughts
close my eyes
Hear the waves
of coming tide

Scent of salt
upon my lips,
Warmth of sun
now touch my skin

Whitecaps crash
conforming land
Now lovers walk
footprint to sand

Majestic seagulls
sing their song
Art of seaweed
felt by all

Sounds appear
now so distant
Eyes still shut
an ocean vision

Natural Beauty

A blade of grass amongst the meadows
Bewildered sight of distant pedals

A fawn approaches
quaint, so slowly
Heartbeat pulsing
sound is motion

The stream it glistens
refreshes those
Parched from travel
nature's trove

The fields are lush
green but void
The wind blows calmly
without a noise

The flowers breath of pollination
Scent of beauty, attracts creation

The Chosen One

Love but a wonder, lost but not found
The meaning
the word
distorted you drown

In hopes of true bliss
some fall to remiss
In search of queen
or son born a prince

Is there a path?
Neither charted or cast
Which leads to the truth
of I soulmate I ask,

And If there is one
truly born to become
Will I then be worthy
to accept and not shun

If I choose to pass
while my heart remain cold
Will destiny hail
reveal you to show

That dreams are not vague
merely thoughts to enslave
But the breath of each life
that brings hunger for pain

Ancient Sky

Though alone for just now, my spirit take flight
In the wings of the battle
I'm the birds of the light

Though trials become many, hardships endured
The strength
solidarity
comes to mind for a word

Must be a strong father
who comfort and cuddle
At night kiss your cheeks
say good nights, and I love you

Stand tall a role model
my daughter, my world
Will never see harm
yes you're daddy's little girl

It is you that I live for
wake up each day
Push forward to triumph
never to stray

I promise you now
as I write on this page
To always be here
through rainiest days

Now this is the bird
I speak of the light
These but the words
that disturb me at night

Though born to be free
oppression seems right
I close my eyes slow
but the walls are still tight

I channel my anger
bottle and ship it
As the clouds of all black
engulf all my vision

The darkness it falls
to the hearts of the soul

Will I be remembered
in the end when I fall

Empathy Not Seen

The walk of hollow
observed as sadness
upon a grain of time

A cardinal past
sang then followed
Pragmatic sounds entwined

At a low
I continue
with melancholy guise

For my affliction
for a sign
the cardinal denied

Lost Traveler

Illumination of shadows
reflect on a past
A time not forgotten
endured to outlast

A city of souls often lost and untold,
Travel silent at night, heart heavy now cold.

Though passage through fate
left an emptiness state
A mind of regret
proved harder to break

Now stuck in a wander
all choices are felt
Lived life as a rebel
left only to self

One contemplates pain
an excuse for the blame
Live life for the moment
or travel in vein

Love Lost

Forget me as now
I am no longer with you
Gone are the moments
we shared I forgive you

Love echos a switch
in defense we turn off
Your actions spoke words
I elected to pause,

For he who knows secrets
the heart whisper knows
The end tells a tale
our strength to let go

Left Alone

The robin spoke at early dawn
Tales of glory far beyond
Eyes now open, yawn aside
Tail to sunrise, wings to glide

No more sight
not one word
Each day I wait
without this bird

Years have past
remain unknown
Robin spoke
then left alone

My Child

My first born son
A first time trying
Tears to eyes, I watch him trying

His heart majestic, soul too sweet
Left alone, the mind to weep

I see your struggle, feel your fear
No worries son, your daddy's here

The fight is now, I'm right here with you
At every step, I walk it with you

I write this message so you can hear it
Emotions running, mind and spirit

With every step, we walk today
I worry more, take me away

Please tell me child, that your ok
My life if lost, while your away

Time...

If I should pass before tomorrow

The seed was sown, whence time was borrowed

The sunrise would forever
have new meaning

The beauty of which, is no longer seeing